P9-CMX-749

3 5674 03535830 9

CHASE BRANCH LIBRARY
17731 W. SEVEN MILE
DETROIT, MICH. 48235

FEB -- 2002

CH

MARTIAL ARTS

Judo

'Highly recommended reading for
any aspiring martial artist.
This series will enhance your
knowledge of styles, history,
grading systems and finding and
analyzing the right club.'

*Stan 'The Man' Longinidis
8-times World Kickboxing
Champion*

PAUL COLLINS

This edition first published in 2002 in the United States of America by
Chelsea House Publishers, a subsidiary of Haights Cross Communications.

All rights reserved. No part of this publication may be reproduced or
transmitted in any form or by any means without the written permission of
the publisher.

Chelsea House Publishers
1974 Sproul Road, Suite 400
Broomall, PA 19008-0914

The Chelsea House world wide web address is www.chelseahouse.com

Library of Congress Cataloging-in-Publication Data Applied for.

ISBN 0-7910-6553-7

First published in 2000 by
Macmillan Education Australia Pty Ltd
627 Chapel Street, South Yarra, Australia, 3141

Copyright © Paul Collins 2000

Text design and page layout by Judith Summerfeldt-Grace
Cover design by Judith Summerfeldt-Grace

Printed in Hong Kong

Acknowledgements
Photographs by Nick Sandalis, except p. 9 © Geostock.

The author would like to thank Mr and Mrs Yamada and their students
from Yamada Judo Academy, 6 Maple Street, Caulfield South, Victoria,
Australia and Bob Todd, 7th Dan and Chairman of the JFA Inc Grades
Commission and member of the Professional Boxing and Martial Arts
Board of Victoria, Australia.

**Techniques used in this book should only be practiced under qualified
supervision.**

Contents

What are martial arts?

Most people have seen at least one fantastic martial arts movie. A lot of it is trick photography. A **ninja** can not really jump backwards and land on the roof of a towering house! Then again, martial arts is about belief — belief in yourself and your ability to overcome any obstacle, no matter how big or small.

Ask any martial arts student why they train and the answer will be to learn **self-defense**. But that answer only scratches the surface of the term 'martial arts'.

One of the many functions of martial arts is to train students, both physically and mentally.

Martial arts has an ancient tradition that is steeped in discipline and dedication. Most martial arts have developed from ancient Asian combat skills. In **feudal** times, people in Asia had to defend themselves against attack. Quite often, peasants were not allowed to carry weapons, so self-defense became their weapon.

Some martial arts are fighting sports, such as karate and kung fu. Other martial arts concentrate on self-improvement, although self-defense is part of the training. These martial arts, like judo and taekwondo, share the syllable *do*. Do means 'the way to **enlightenment**'.

The main martial arts

Aikido (Japan)

Hapkido (Korea)

Judo (Japan)

Jujitsu (Japan)

Karate (Japan)

Kendo (Japan)

Kung fu (China)

Muay Thai/Kickboxing (Thailand)

Ninjutsu (Japan)

Samurai (Japan)

Sumo wrestling (Japan)

Taekwondo (Korea)

Tai Chi (China)

Kung fu

Taekwondo

Karate

Dedication and discipline

Judo is hard work. Ask any senior student. On average, it takes at least three-and-a-half years to reach black belt status, and even then there is a lot more to learn.

Dedication plays a major role in the life of a martial arts student. Training can be up to four times a week, and an average session lasts from 60 to 90 minutes.

Students practice one simple procedure over and over again. They might repeat a simple move 20 times in one night, only to repeat the same move the next time they train. Martial artists learn through repetition, so that even the most basic moves can be automatically performed when they are suddenly required.

Some martial artists will even die for their art. Take Gunji Koizumi for instance. He was the founder of British judo and a dedicated instructor. At the age of 80, he decided to die in the manner of the old samurai and committed **hara kiri**.

It's a fact!

Judo

Understanding judo

Judo is often referred to as a physical game of chess. This is because each opponent must study the other's weaknesses and take advantage of them. Judo uses opposites of balance such as **Yin and Yang**, the two basic principles of the universe in Chinese philosophy. Yin is passive and yielding, whereas Yang is active and assertive.

In judo, the idea is to put your opponent on the ground with little effort. One opponent may push, and the other will resist. Suddenly, the person resisting will give way and use their opponent's strength against them.

Immobilization techniques used in judo are strangleholds, armlocks, body throws and hold downs. Other methods include foot sweeps and falls. Usually only senior students, aged 16-plus, use the more serious techniques. There are no legal kicks or punches in the junior levels, although more advanced students do practice them.

Unlike other martial arts, judo is the same all over the world. There are no different styles in judo like there are in karate and taekwondo.

*The Yin and Yang emblem is known to most martial artists. The Yin and the Yang represent the feminine and the masculine energies in martial arts. The Yin can be explained as flowing and fluid, as in performing patterns and good technique. The Yang might be the power and the force of **sparring** with a partner. Martial arts need both opposing energies, the Yin and the Yang.*

Getting to grips. Before unbalancing an opponent, a judoka, or judo player, must have a firm grip on their opponent's uniform. The state of play can be directed to either side, backward or forward with this standard grip.

It's a fact!

Judo is practiced in over 100 countries.

Japan: the birthplace of judo

Population:	126.2 million
Language:	Japanese
Currency:	Yen (¥)
Main Religions:	Shinto, Buddhism and Christianity

Japan leads the world as a fishing nation. This is because it is a nation of mountainous islands in the North Pacific Ocean. The four main islands are Honshu, Kyushu, Shikoku and Hokkaido, and they are situated off the mainland of east Asia. Tokyo, on the island of Honshu, is the capital city of Japan.

Many of Japan's mountains are active volcanoes, which often cause earthquakes. Mount Fuji is Japan's tallest mountain. It is 3,776 meters (12,390 feet) high and it is an extinct, or dormant, volcano.

The government of Japan is a democratic government, elected by the people. The head of government is the Prime Minister. The Emperor of Japan is the ceremonial head of state.

Kyushu

Shikoku

Pacific Ocean

8

Hokkaido

Sea of Japan

Honshu

Mount Fuji

■ Tokyo

Miyajima Island, Japan.

Pacific Ocean

In 1945, after Japan's surrender to the Allied Forces in WWII, judo and other martial arts were banned in Japan by the Allied Commission.

It's a fact!

The history of judo

It's a fact!

The most successful female judoka is Ingrid Berghmans from Belgium. She has won six world titles.

The founder of modern judo was Master Jigoro Kano (1860-1938). When he was 11, Kano's family moved to Tokyo from the country. Because he was new in town, Kano was picked on by bullies. He took up an ancient feudal Japanese fighting art called jujitsu. He became quite good at it and the bullies left him alone.

Kano continued studying jujitsu and then formed his own style, which became known as Kodokan judo. It was not long before the jujitsu masters around Japan became jealous and questioned Kano's teachings. Finally there was a showdown: Kodokan judo versus jujitsu.

The tournament proved a great success for Kano, whose team defeated the jujitsu team. Kano opened his first dojo (training hall) in 1882, and judo became very popular in Japan.

Kano and his leading pupil, Yukio Tani, went to Europe in 1889. Tani gave his first martial arts display in Britain and the sport was taught to French police. In the early 1900s, another of Kano's pupils, Yashiro Yamashita, introduced judo into the United States. One of *his* students was President Theodore Roosevelt!

Yamashita is the sport's most successful judoka. He won nine Japanese titles and four world titles in the heavyweight division. When Yamashita retired in 1985, he was undefeated after 203 consecutive wins.

The sport became best-known when Tokyo hosted the 1964 Olympic Games and requested that judo be included as a demonstration sport. Judo has been a permanent sport at Olympic games since 1972 for men and since 1992 for women.

Dress code and etiquette

Dress code

The judo uniform is called a judogi. Like most other martial arts uniforms, a judogi looks like loose-fitting white pajamas with a belt around the waist.

The judogi is made from cotton and is designed to withstand training and contests. The various parts of the judogi that are target areas for gripping (lapels, collar and armpits) are reinforced and often have extra panels sewn in for protection. There are no zips, buttons or pockets that might cause injury.

A judogi. Judo uniforms are tougher than other martial arts uniforms. The pants are tied with a drawstring. The top folds left over right and is tied with a belt.

How to tie your belt

1 *Hold the belt across the front of your waist, with both ends equal length on either side.*

2 *Pass both ends of the belt around your body.*

3 *Cross the left end of the belt over the right end.*

4 *Tuck the right end of the belt under the middle of the belt.*

5 *Tie the ends together, right over left (this is a reef knot).*

6 *Pull tight.*

Etiquette

- Bow when entering or leaving a dojo. Bowing at the start and end of a contest is also a sign of respect for your opponent or the instructor.

- Your uniform must always be well-kept and clean.

- Fingernails and toenails should always be trimmed. Long nails can cause injury to both yourself and your opponent. Judo techniques involve gripping an opponent's jacket so long fingernails can be torn when a grip is broken.

- Jewelry, such as earrings and necklaces, is not worn while performing, as it can cause injury if it becomes snagged.

- When giving in to a hold that you are unable to break from, you should sharply tap your opponent twice with the flat of your hand. You can submit verbally only if you are unable to move a hand.

- Never take advantage of lesser **ranks**. This will not be tolerated in any club. It is considered a disgrace to injure anyone while practicing judo.

- Footwear is not allowed to be worn on the mats. Some clubs insist that zori (sandals)must be worn while off the mats.

- Students should never idly chatter among themselves or distract other students who are training.

- Eating and drinking are not permitted in the dojo.

1 Stand with your palms on your thighs.

2 Bow from the waist, sliding your hands down over your knees.

Kneeling bow (zarei)
This bow is usually performed before practicing groundwork.

1 Resting on your knees, place your palms on your thighs.

2 Lean forward, placing your hands on the mat in front of your knees.

Before you start

Choosing a club

As judo is the same all over the world you can attend any club and the training will be familiar.

A look through the telephone book under the general heading 'Martial Arts' will show you where the nearest clubs are. It is better to join a large club with many members. Also ensure that the club has students about your own age. If not, you could always join with a friend.

If money is a consideration, phone around and compare costs. They should not vary much. Some clubs have monthly charges, which can work out cheaper if you intend to practice at least twice a week. Other clubs charge a mat fee, or joining fee. Visitors normally do not pay, so it is a good idea to sit in on a session or two before joining a club. Some clubs even offer free introductory classes. As you advance through the grades, a grading fee is charged. Costs vary, depending on the level of grading.

It is better to join a club that has students about your own age.

Clothing

It is not expensive to start judo. Your first few training sessions can be performed in a sweatsuit or loose pants and a T-shirt. Apart from the judogi, the only other gear the judoka may need are zori, for walking to or from the mat area.

Before paying for a new judo uniform, visit second-hand or recycled clothing stores. Be sure to specify that you require a judo uniform. You could even ask the club that you are joining if any older students have uniforms that are now too small for them. This will also save you from having to buy the club's badges and sew them on.

If you buy your uniform new, be sure to order it one size too big. Despite what the manufacturer's label says, the uniforms do shrink.

You will also need to purchase your new club's badges and the correct belt for your judogi.

'He who hangs on is certain
not hang on need have n

16

Insurance

Insurance is advised, although you are unlikely to get badly injured at a well-run judo club. Most clubs have insurance cover so it pays to ask.

Confidence and disabilities

Everyone feels nervous when they first enter a dojo under bright lights. Once you have passed your first few belt gradings — everyone passes the early belts — you will feel more confident. If you push yourself to face your fears, it will be easier to overcome them.

A light stretching work-out just before competition is a good way to keep warm and to loosen stiff muscles, which can cause nerves. Good instructors will teach you breathing techniques, which will calm you and help you to focus.

A disability should not stop you from trying judo. Many top athletes have **asthma**. Other athletes have **diabetes**. Getting fit through judo can help improve your overall condition. Just make sure your instructor knows of your complaint, take the necessary precautions and bow out when you do not feel well.

to fall, but he who does
fear of falling.'

Anonymous

17

Fitness and training

Beginner martial artists are not usually ready for serious training. This takes time. They need to build fitness slowly. Most martial arts clubs have a beginners' class, where students learn the basic self-defense techniques and get fit.

At the start of each training session, students bow to their instructor. A warm-up follows which involves stretching exercises. The instructor will then teach the class something new or ask the class to practice techniques already learned.

Contests are sometimes part of a training session, and some instructors pick teams to compete against one another.

Stretching

As well as fitness you will need to gain flexibility. This means stretching all your body parts. You need to loosen and warm tight and cold muscles.

It is important to keep each stretching movement gentle and slow. You should not use jerking or bouncing movements.

It is equally important to cool down after exercising. This maintains the level of blood circulation and reduces muscle spasms. Gentle cool-down stretches also help prevent injuries, because they reduce muscle tightness.

Stretching has many purposes. It:
- increases heart and lung capacity
- helps you practice for the movements you are about to perform
- helps avoid injury from pulled muscles
- gives you greater flexibility.

Stretching exercises

1 Groin stretch

2 Back stretch

3 Back stretch

4 Shoulder stretch

5 Hamstring stretch

Fitness games

There are many fitness games young judo students play. These are used as warm-ups and warm-downs, as well as breaks from hard training. Some fitness games include skipping from side to side over a belt held by two partners, jumping in the air and twisting your body at the same time, and tug-of-war.

Fitness game: Crab Crawl.
Crawling forward on hands and feet is harder than it looks. It certainly tests your fitness.

Sparring

Sparring is where students pair off and exchange techniques with each other, usually without knowing their partner's next move. Sparring is practiced in training and it is a way of practicing moves that have been learned. Sparring is not competitive as there is no winner or loser. The rules for sparring are set by the instructor.

Fitness game: The Tunnel.
Starting at one end of the 'tunnel', a student crawls to the other end and forms part of the tunnel, while the next student crawls down.

Fitness game: Forward Crab Crawl.
This game is a good warm-up exercise.

Sparring

'Judo is a training for life.'

Master Jigoro Kano

Judo techniques

Judo techniques are split into three main groups: throws, holds, and armlocks and strangleholds.

Throws

There are about 50 throws in judo. These are done by unbalancing an opponent and applying leverage or force to throw them. Judo translated means 'gentle way' or 'way of flexibility'.

Rather than pull back when an opponent grabs you, the idea is to give in to that pull and not resist it. By doing this, you unbalance your opponent because they expect you to pull back.

A one-handed shoulder throw

1 *Hook one arm under your opponent's armpit.*

Holds

A scarf hold

There are up to ten basic holds. Once you have your opponent on the mat, you apply pressure. Your opponent should tap either you or the mat in submission if they are unable to break the hold.

1 *Place one arm around your opponent's neck and hold their free arm at the elbow. Spread your legs for firm balance.*

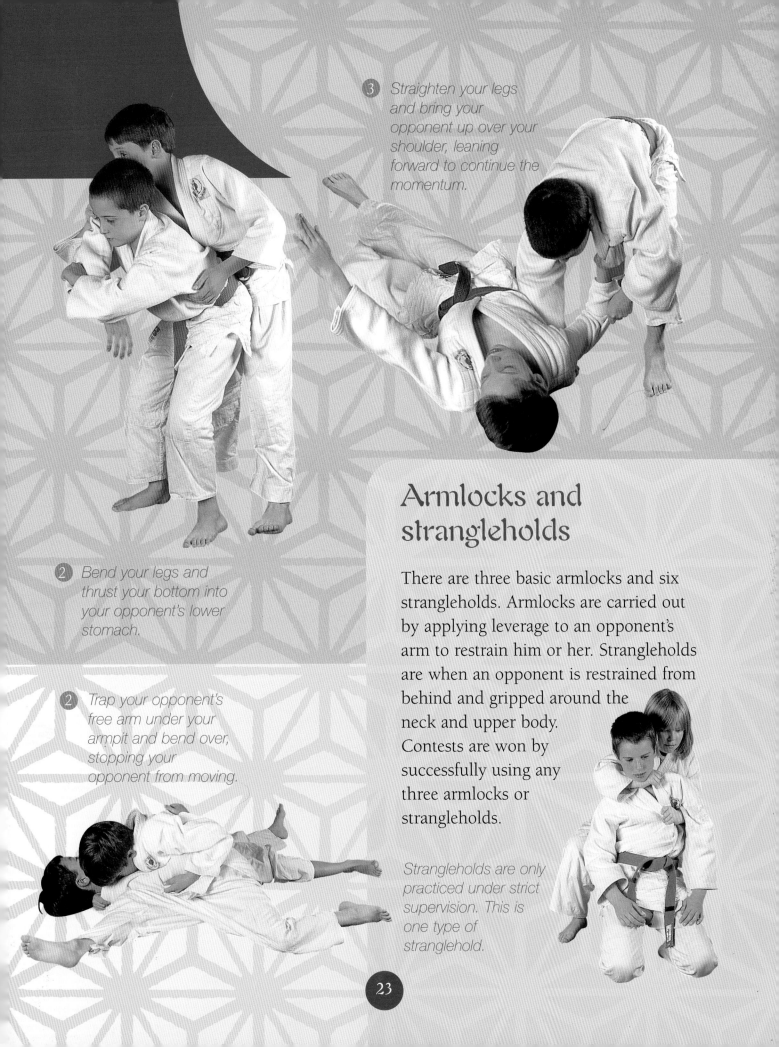

③ Straighten your legs and bring your opponent up over your shoulder, leaning forward to continue the momentum.

② Bend your legs and thrust your bottom into your opponent's lower stomach.

② Trap your opponent's free arm under your armpit and bend over, stopping your opponent from moving.

Armlocks and strangleholds

There are three basic armlocks and six strangleholds. Armlocks are carried out by applying leverage to an opponent's arm to restrain him or her. Strangleholds are when an opponent is restrained from behind and gripped around the neck and upper body. Contests are won by successfully using any three armlocks or strangleholds.

Strangleholds are only practiced under strict supervision. This is one type of stranglehold.

Breakfalls

To avoid being injured in judo it is important to break a fall correctly, with arms outstretched. There are basically four types of breakfalls:

- ⊙ to the front
- ⊙ to the side
- ⊙ backwards
- ⊙ over the shoulder.

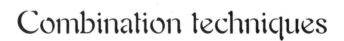

Rolling breakfall to the side

1 *With feet apart, bend slightly into your proposed fall.*

Combination techniques

Single techniques do not always work, especially if your opponent is as experienced as you are. Therefore a series of moves may be essential. These are called combination techniques.

For example, if you successfully block an opponent's punch, your opponent might then counter your defense by clasping your wrist. You then need to break from the wristlock and perform another technique.

② *Place your hands as pictured.*

③ *Keep your head down and let yourself roll naturally over your arm and shoulder.*

④ *When you come out of the roll, hit the mat with your hand and arm flush against the mat.*

Kata (forms)

Judo **kata** are a series of movements, known as forms or patterns. They are performed with a partner and are structured around moves such as throws or sweeps (sweeping the foot from under your opponent). Kata are designed to practice skills that have been learned.

The belt system

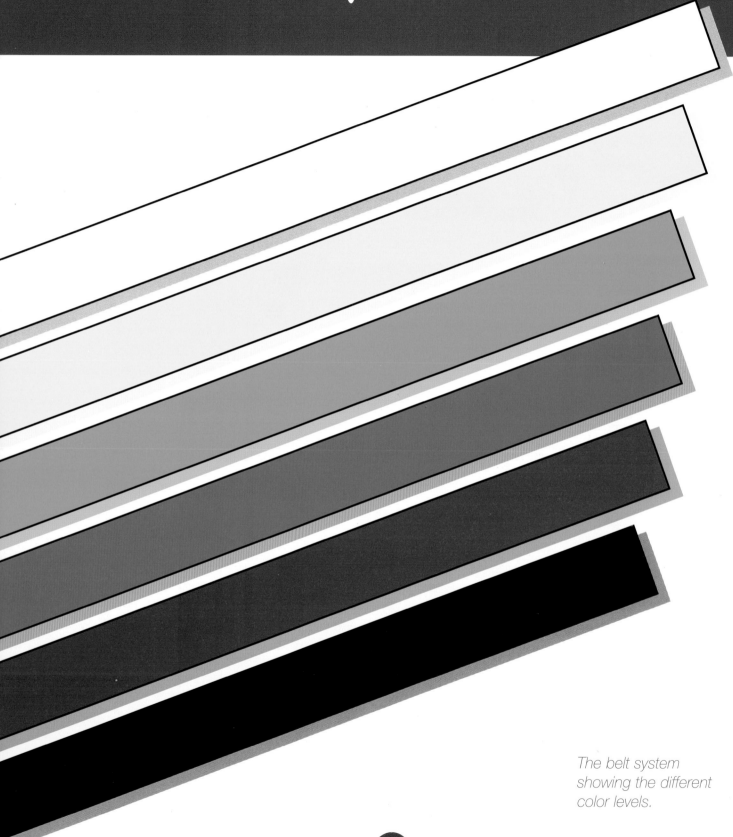

The belt system showing the different color levels.

26

The color of a judoka's belt indicates the standard the wearer has reached. Most martial arts have a belt system but the colors of achievement often vary.

In judo, white belts are worn by beginners and black belts are worn by masters. Grades in-between wear other colors. For each color level there are different grades that students have to pass. White stripes are added to the colored belts to indicate the grade a student has achieved.

Once you have reached black belt ability, you move on to dans. You wear a black belt until you reach fifth dan. Sixth, seventh and eighth dans wear red and white striped belts. Ninth and tenth dans wear a red belt.

To achieve a higher grading, students sometimes have to compete in a contest, although their grading is not judged on the outcome. Many clubs also require students to perform 40 throws and 40 groundwork movements and some kata work before moving on to the next grade. Examiners judge the students' performances.

Only seven judo practitioners ever reached 10th dan.

It's a fact!

The language of judo

In judo, major commands are spoken in Japanese. It is a sign of respect to know Japanese, since judo originated in Japan. A judo player can also travel anywhere in the world and understand the language of judo.

Japanese words sound the way they are written. For instance, 'judogi' is pronounced 'joo-doe-gee' and 'Sensei' is pronounced 'sen-say'. 'G' is pronounced like the 'g' in 'get', not like the 'g' in 'gentle'. 'I' is pronounced 'ee'.

The following are words that you may learn when studying judo.

dan	step (black belt grade)
dojo	training hall
hajime	begin
ippon	full point (equals ten small points)
judogi	judo suit
judoka	judo player
kata	form or pattern of movements developed to improve technique by repetition
koka	a point that is less than a yuko (a three-point score)
kyu	senior grade
mon	junior grade
nagewaza	throws
obi	belt
osaekomi	the word the timekeeper uses to begin the count in a contest

It's a fact!

Many Japanese words are interpreted as either singular or plural. For instance, the plural of 'dojo' is dojo and the plural of 'samurai' is still samurai.

28

randori	sparring/practice	
rei	bow	
ritsurei	standing bow	
sensei	teacher	
shiai	competition	
tatami	practice mat (traditionally rice straw mat)	
tori	attacker	
uchikomi	sparring with partner	
uke	defender	
ukemi	breakfall	
waza-ari	near point	
yuko	a score between a small point and a near point	
zarei	kneeling bow	
zori	traditional Japanese sandals	

Counting one to ten

ichi	one	1
ni	two	2
san	three	3
shi	four	4
go	five	5
roku	six	6
shichi	seven	7
hachi	eight	8
ku	nine	9
ju	ten	10

Competition

Championships are held in big halls. Two judges, who sit in opposite corners, a referee, a timekeeper and a scorer preside over matches.

The contest area is either eight or ten meters square (12 square yards), surrounded by a throw-off area of three meters (9.8 feet). The outer edge of the contest area is a meter (3.2 feet) wide and is red. This area is known as the danger area because it is a warning that you are in danger of stepping off the mat.

Judo matches are won by pinning an opponent to the mat for 25 seconds. Judo fights last four minutes for women and five minutes for men.

'Osaekomi' indicates that a successful hold-down is in place and that the countdown should begin.

Points are scored depending upon how successful a technique is demonstrated.

Winners can win outright by scoring ten points or by scoring two lots of seven points. If neither contestant scores these points, the judges decide which contestant attacked the most and declare them as the winner.

A referee's signals

1. Ippon   2. Waza-ari   3. Yuko   4. Koka   5. Osaekomi

Glossary

armlock	applying leverage to an opponent's arm to restrain him or her	ninja	traditionally a spy or assassin
asthma	a breathing disorder	rank	the level of achievement you have reached
diabetes	a disease where the body does not fully take in sugar	self-defense	usually grappling, which involves pinning your opponent so they cannot strike you
enlightenment	well-informed		
feudal	dating back to the Middle Ages	sparring	exchanging techniques with a partner, usually without the partner knowing the next move
hara kiri	ritual suicide (ripping open the abdomen using a knife)		
		stance	a feet and leg position
immobilize	to hold still or stop movement	submit	to give up when in a hold that you are unable to get out of
jujitsu	a form of unarmed combat, created before judo		
		Yin and Yang	the two basic principles of the universe in Chinese philosophy. Yin is passive and yielding, whereas Yang is active and assertive
kata	a series of movements designed to practice techniques that have been learned		

Index